Handmade THANKSGIVING Crafts

By Ruth Owen

 Gareth Stevens
PUBLISHING

Please visit our website, www.garethstevens.com. For a free color catalog of all our high-quality books, call toll free 1-800-542-2595 or fax 1-877-542-2596.

Cataloging-in-Publication Data
Names: Owen, Ruth.
Title: Handmade Thanksgiving crafts / Ruth Owen.
Description: New York : Gareth Stevens Publishing, 2017. | Series: Handmade holiday crafts | Includes index.
Identifiers: ISBN 9781482460896 (pbk.) | ISBN 9781482461596 (library bound) | ISBN 9781482460902 (6 pack)
Subjects: LCSH: Thanksgiving decorations--Juvenile literature. | Handicraft--Juvenile literature.
Classification: LCC TT900.T5 O84 2017 | DDC 745.594'1649--dc23

Published in 2017 by
Gareth Stevens Publishing
111 East 14th Street, Suite 349
New York, NY 10003

Copyright © 2017 Gareth Stevens Publishing

First Edition

Produced for Gareth Stevens Publishing by Ruby Tuesday Books Ltd
Designer: Emma Randall

Photo Credits: Courtesy of Ruby Tuesday Books and Shutterstock.

Printed in the United States of America
CPSIA compliance information: Batch CW17GS:
For further information contact Gareth Stevens, New York, New York at 1-800-542-2595.

CONTENTS

A HAPPY HANDMADE HOLIDAY

When family and friends visit at Thanksgiving this year, impress them with your **creativity** and crafting skills.

From place settings to napkin rings, and table decorations to a Thanksgiving wreath, this book includes projects that can be made using inexpensive craft supplies and scraps of **recycled** materials from around your home.

All you need to do is follow the instructions, and you'll soon be having a very happy handmade Thanksgiving!

STAY SAFE

It's very important to have an adult around whenever you do any of the following tasks:

• Use scissors

• Use a craft knife

• Use a glue gun

YOU WILL NEED:

To make the projects in this book, you don't need any special equipment—just some basic crafting tools and supplies.

- Scissors
- Glue gun
- White glue
- Paints and paintbrushes
- Stapler
- A craft knife
- A hole punch
- A ruler
- A measuring tape

TABLETOP TURKEY

You'll need three to four days to create this **papier-mâché** turkey decoration. It's worth it, though, and can be used as a cute centerpiece for your family's Thanksgiving dinner.

YOU WILL NEED:

- A newspaper
- Extra newspaper to protect your table or countertop
- Two balloons
- Cooking oil
- White glue (mixed three parts glue to one part water)
- A paintbrush
- Black marker
- A craft knife
- A toilet paper tube
- Three cups of dry sand or pebbles
- Tape
- White and brown paint
- Cardboard in various colors and patterns
- Scissors
- A glue gun
- Googly eyes
- A small piece of red fabric or felt

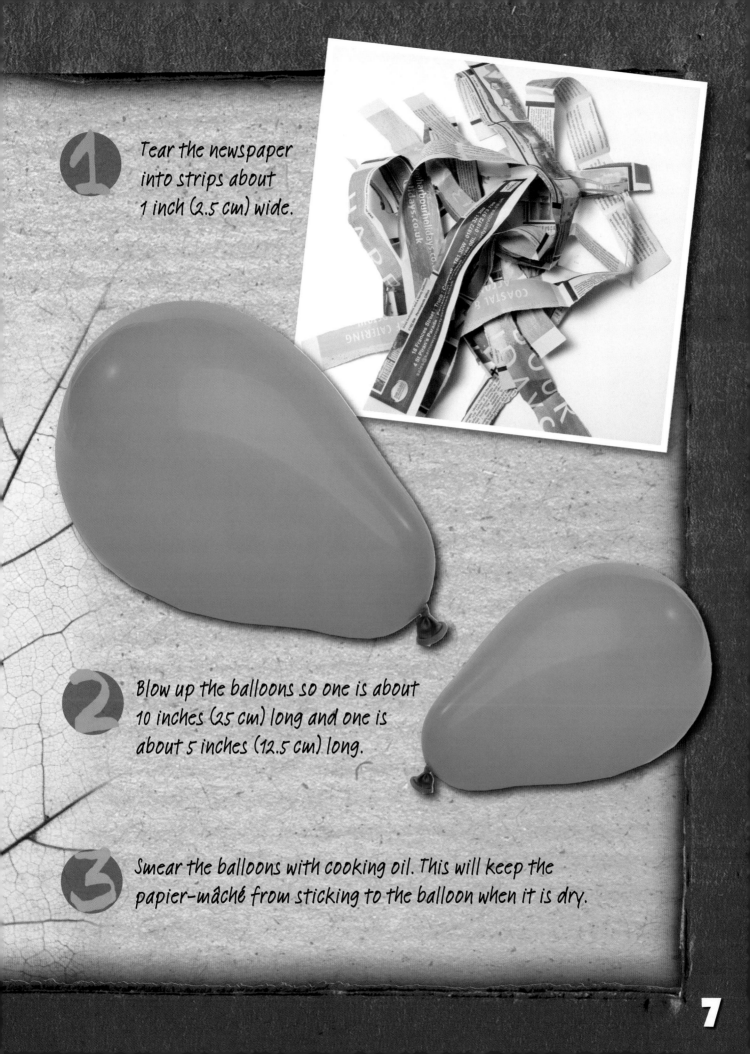

1 Tear the newspaper into strips about 1 inch (2.5 cm) wide.

2 Blow up the balloons so one is about 10 inches (25 cm) long and one is about 5 inches (12.5 cm) long.

3 Smear the balloons with cooking oil. This will keep the papier-mâché from sticking to the balloon when it is dry.

7

4 Using the paintbrush, brush some of the glue mixture onto the large balloon. Lay a strip of newspaper onto the glue, and then brush more glue over the top. Repeat this with more newspaper strips, slightly overlapping each strip, until the balloon is covered and only the knot can be seen.

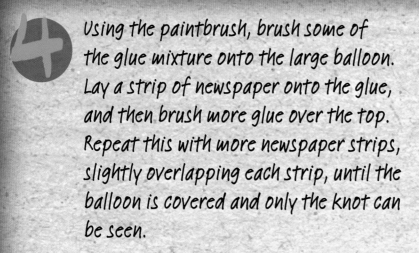

5 Repeat step 4 on the small balloon. Then, allow the papier-mâché to dry for 24 hours.

6 Add a second layer of newspaper strips to each balloon and allow to dry for 24 hours. Then add a third layer and allow to dry for 24 hours.

7 Place the end of the toilet paper tube over the knotted end of the large balloon. Trace a circle onto the papier-mâché. Repeat for the small balloon. Cut out the two circles, popping and pulling out the balloons.

8 Pour the sand or pebbles into the turkey's body so it stands up by itself.

9 Use the toilet paper tube as a neck to join the body to the head and tape in place. Then cover the neck and tape with a layer of papier-mâché. Allow to dry.

Paint the turkey white to cover all the newspaper. When dry, paint the turkey brown.

Tail feathers

Wings

11 Cut tail feathers and wings from colorful cardboard.

12 Make a cone-shaped beak from a small piece of thick paper or cardboard. Cut a long, thin teardrop shape from the red fabric to make the turkey's snood.

Cardboard tail feathers

Snood

Cardboard wing

When the paint is dry, use the glue gun to stick on the tail feathers, wings, beak, snood, and googly eyes. Your turkey is ready to gobble-gobble!

BUBBLE WRAP CORN DECORATIONS

These cute bubble wrap corn decorations will look great decorating your home for Thanksgiving!

YOU WILL NEED:

- Yellow card stock
- Scissors
- Bubble wrap
- White glue
- Paint suitable for use on plastic
- Paintbrushes
- Brown paper
- A hole punch
- Raffia string

Begin by cutting an oval corncob shape from the yellow card stock. Then use this piece of card stock as a template.

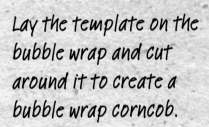

Lay the template on the bubble wrap and cut around it to create a bubble wrap corncob.

 Glue the bubble wrap to the card stock.

 Paint the bubble wrap yellow, orange, or brown.

4 When the base coat of paint is dry, paint some of the bubbles in contrasting colors, such as orange, blue, red, and black, to create the dried corn effect.

5 As the corncob dries, cut two long leaves from the brown paper.

Glue the brown paper leaves to the back of the corncob. Finally, punch a hole through the bottom of the corncob.

 Now make a second corncob. Then thread raffia string through the punched holes in the two corncobs and tie in a bow.

EASY PAPER PUMPKINS

Pumpkins are a **traditional** decoration at Thanksgiving. So decorate your home and Thanksgiving dinner table with some easy-to-make paper pumpkins.

YOU WILL NEED:

- Orange craft paper
- Green craft paper
- Ruler
- Scissors
- Stapler or white glue
- A toothpick or wooden skewer

To make your pumpkins extra decorative, you can buy patterned craft paper, or lacy stamped paper strips as shown here.

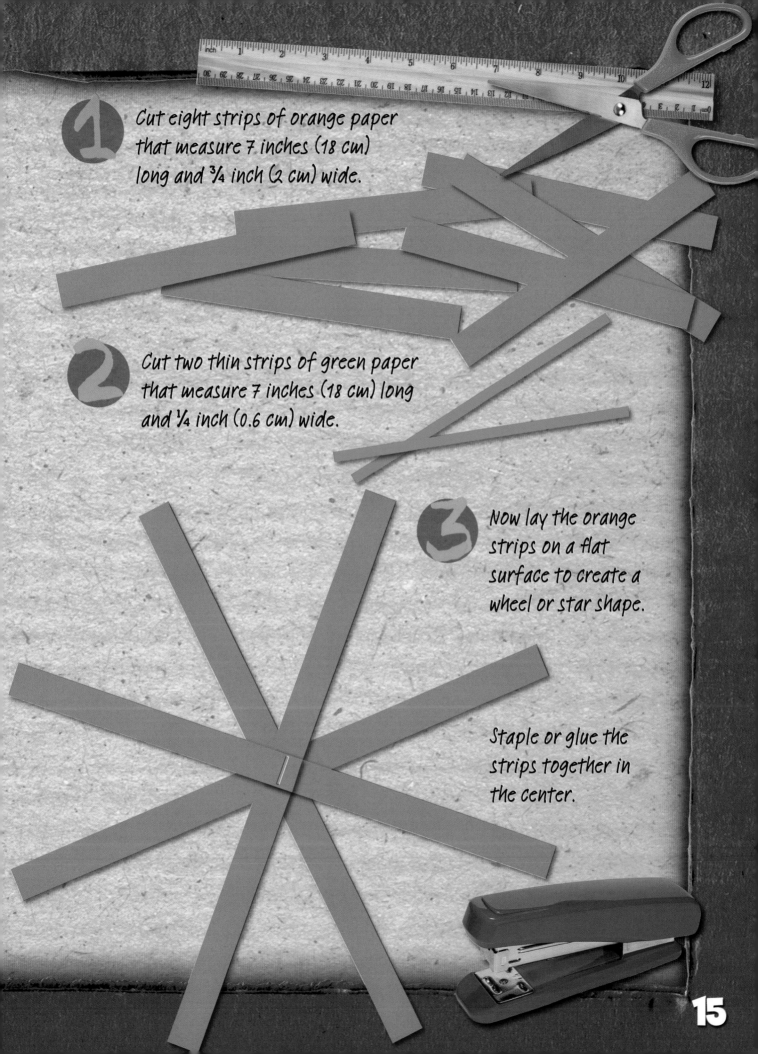

1 Cut eight strips of orange paper that measure 7 inches (18 cm) long and ¾ inch (2 cm) wide.

2 Cut two thin strips of green paper that measure 7 inches (18 cm) long and ¼ inch (0.6 cm) wide.

3 Now lay the orange strips on a flat surface to create a wheel or star shape.

Staple or glue the strips together in the center.

15

4 Gather the other ends of the strips together and glue or staple them. Before you join them, make sure they are evenly spaced and make a good, rounded shape.

5 Next, cut out a leaf shape from the green paper.

6 To make a pumpkin's curly tendrils, take one of the thin green strips of paper and wind it tightly around a toothpick.

Slide the coil of paper off the toothpick and it will curl up. Repeat with the second strip of green paper.

The art of curling and folding paper into shapes and pictures is called **quilling.**

7 Finally, glue or staple the leaf and the two tendrils to the top of the pumpkin.

make a fold in the tendril

To make a long tendril, slightly unroll one of the coils and make a small fold in its length to stop it from curling back up.

TURKEY LEG PLACE SETTINGS

These fun turkey leg place settings are packed with treats to eat and will get everyone around the table smiling.

YOU WILL NEED:

To make each place setting
- White cardboard
- A pencil
- Scissors
- Colored paper
- A small brown paper lunch bag
- Popcorn and autumn candy
- A glue gun
- White glue

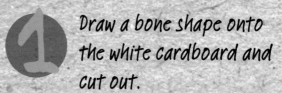

1 Draw a bone shape onto the white cardboard and cut out.

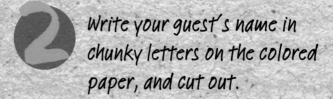

2 Write your guest's name in chunky letters on the colored paper, and cut out.

TOM

3 Take a brown paper bag and fill it with popcorn and candy.

4 Scrunch and shape the bag to make it into a rounded shape. Then gather up the neck of the bag, insert the white cardboard bone, and glue it in place.

5 Finally, glue your guest's name to the paper bag turkey leg.

PONY BEAD NAPKIN RINGS

All you need to create your own set of **unique** handmade napkin rings is some string and pony beads.

YOU WILL NEED:

- String
- Measuring tape
- Pony beads
- Scissors

Choose beads in orange, yellow, and other natural autumn colors to create a dried corncob effect for your napkin rings.

1 Measure and cut a piece of string that is about 4 feet (1.2 m) long.

2 Take four beads and thread them onto the string.

3 Now take hold of the left-hand side of the string and thread it through the beads from right to left.

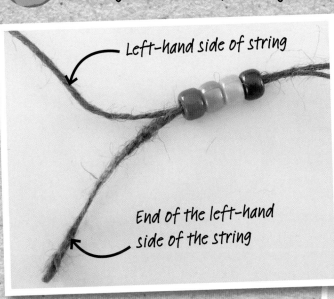

Left-hand side of string

End of the left-hand side of the string

Then pull on both ends of the string to tighten up the loop that's been formed.

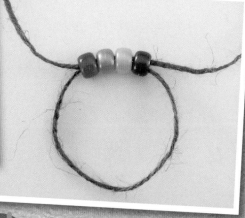

First row of beads

Loop you made in Step 3

Right-hand side of the string

4 Now take hold of the right-hand side of the string and thread on the next row of four beads.

On this second row, reverse the order of the beads.

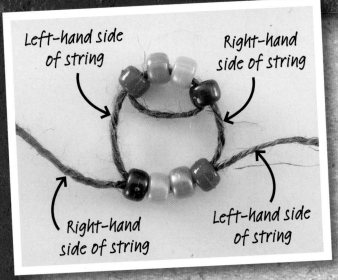

Left-hand side of string

Right-hand side of string

Right-hand side of string

Left-hand side of string

5 Next, thread the left-hand side of the string through the second row of beads from left to right, and tighten the loop.

6 Now take hold of the string on the left-hand side and thread on the next four beads.

Then thread the string on the right-hand side back through the third row of beads from right to left, and tighten.

As you work, the ends of the string may get a little fuzzy and difficult to thread, so just trim off a tiny amount to make the ends sharp again.

7 Keep repeating the steps until you've threaded 12 rows of beads.

Now take hold of the left-hand side of the string. Thread it from left to right through the first row of beads.

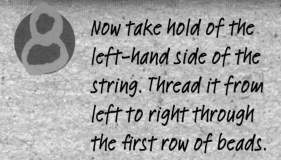

Then take hold of the right-hand piece of string and thread it right to left through the first row of beads.

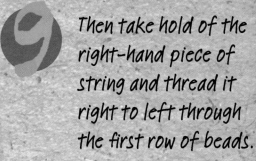

Take hold of both ends of the string and pull. As you tighten the string, the beads will curl up and form a ring.

Then tie the two sides of the string into a double knot inside the ring and trim off any spare string.

Your napkin ring is complete!

THANK-YOU WREATH

Make this beautiful wreath of paper autumn leaves and invite your friends and family to say "Thank You!" for everything that's important in their lives.

2-D leaves

The paper leaves are a combination of flat **two-dimensional (2-D)** leaves and **origami** leaves.

Origami leaves

YOU WILL NEED:

- 12-inch (30.5 cm) foam wreath frame
- Tracing paper
- A pencil
- Scissors
- Thin card stock in autumn colors
- Origami or craft paper in autumn colors
- Glue gun
- A black marker
- Pins

Soccer

My teacher

Mom and Dad

My friends

1 You can buy foam wreath shapes from craft stores, garden centers, and florists.

2 To make the 2-D leaves, trace these three leaf shapes and cut them out.

3 Lay the tracing paper leaf shapes on the colored card stock and draw around them. Then cut out the leaves. At this stage, make about 15 leaves.

To make an origami leaf, place a sheet of origami paper colored side down. Fold the paper diagonally, and crease.

 Fold the top and bottom points into the center fold, and crease.

Then fold the model in half.

 Make a fold at one end of the model.

Now turn the model over and make a fold in the other direction.

Use the first fold as a marker for the size of the second folded part.

7 Turn the model back over and make another fold. Keep turning and folding.

When all the paper is folded, your model should look like this.

8 Finally, take hold of both ends of the model and gently pull in opposite directions to open out the folds. Then unfold the leaf. Make about 10 to 15 origami leaves.

Now put your wreath together. Using a glue gun, stick the 2-D and origami leaves to the wreath frame.

If you wish, you can collect real fallen leaves. Allow them to dry out and then glue them to your wreath.

10 When the wreath is complete, make some more 2-D leaves and use these to write your Thanksgiving gratitude messages.

Think about the things you're thankful for and write them on a leaf.

Mom and Dad

Soccer

My teacher

My friends

11 Pin these leaves to your wreath. When friends or family visit at Thanksgiving, ask them to write their own thank-you messages and pin them to the wreath, too.

GLOSSARY

creativity
The use of imagination or original ideas to create something new and unusual.

origami
The art of folding paper into decorative shapes or objects.

papier-mâché
A material made from newspapers and glue that can be molded when it is wet. Papier-mâché hardens as it dries, so it can be used for making models.

quilling
A crafting technique in which narrow strips of paper are wound around a thin tool to create coils of paper. The coils are then arranged to create pictures.

recycled
Objects or materials that have been turned into
something new instead of being thrown away.

rustic
Something that looks plain, simple, and sometimes
old-fashioned.

traditional
A way of thinking, behaving, or doing something that
a group of people have followed for a long time. For
example, making Thanksgiving decorations from
produce such as pumpkins and corn is a tradition.

two-dimensional (2-D)
Something that is flat and has length and width but
no depth.

unique
Something that is one of a kind. Handmade objects
are unique because each one is different from the
next, unlike objects made in a factory.

INDEX

FURTHER INFORMATION

BOOKS:

Eick, Jean. *Thanksgiving Crafts*. Mankato, MN: RiverStream Publishing, 2014.

Muehlenhardt, Amy Bailey. *Thanksgiving Crafts*. North Mankato, MN: Picture Window Books, 2011.

WEBSITES:

http://www.allcrafts.net/thanksgiving.htm
Check out 100 more Thanksgiving handicrafts.